GW00402064

Montgomery of Alamein

Eva Bailey

Illustrated by
Catherine Bradbury

Hamish Hamilton
London

First published 1985 by
Hamish Hamilton Children's Books
Garden House, 57-59 Long Acre, London WC2E 9JZ
Text copyright © 1985 by Eva Bailey
Illustrations copyright © 1985 by Catherine Bradbury
All rights reserved
British Library Cataloguing in Publication Data
Bailey, Eva
Montgomery of Alamein.—(Profiles)
1. Montgomery of Alamein, Bernard Law Montgomery, *Viscount*—
Juvenile literature
2. Great Britain. *Army*—Biography—Juvenile literature
3. Generals—Great Britain—Biography—Juvenile literature
I. Title
355.3'31'0924   DA69.3.M56
ISBN 0-241-11562-0
Typeset by Pioneer
Printed in Great Britain at the
University Press, Cambridge

Contents

Bernard Montgomery, aged three, in the garden of his family's home
in Tasmania

1 Tasmania and London

Bernard Law Montgomery was a naughty little boy. He was defiant and determined, wilful and obstinate. Yet it was these qualities, properly harnessed, which helped to make him the great army commander of World War Two.

Bernard was one of a large family. He was born on 17th November 1887. He had two older brothers and a sister. Eventually there were to be nine children in the family, but one sister and one brother died while they were young.

Bernard's father, the Reverend Henry Montgomery, was a clergyman. He was the Vicar of St Mark's Church in Kennington, London. Bernard's mother, whose name was Maud, was the daughter of Frederick William Farrar, also a clergyman. He was famous for his many writings. One of Grandfather Farrar's works was the novel *Eric, or Little by Little*. Later, while he was the Headmaster of Marlborough College, Dr Farrar wrote *The Life of Christ*, which became a bestseller in Victorian times.

Before Bernard was two years old, his father became the Bishop of Tasmania. In October 1889, the whole of the family at that time — father, mother and five young children — sailed to Tasmania, the small island to the south of Australia. They settled in the capital city, Hobart.

Bernard's father, now Bishop Montgomery, was a very busy man. He was often away from home for months at a time. Bernard's mother was very strict. She had to be, with so many young children to look after. Family prayers, which everyone attended, were held twice a day. The children were made to get up early in the morning and tidy their rooms.

Bernard did not like this stern discipline. He wanted to do just as he pleased. He was disobedient and did things that were not allowed. He always seemed to be in trouble. His two elder brothers were obedient and did as they were told, but Bernard was a rebel. Like his mother, he was very strong-willed and insisted on having his own way. His personality clashed with hers and they frequently quarrelled. Bernard's mother punished her young son for each act of misbehaviour, but he went on being the naughty boy of the family.

Aged nine.

This was not a passing childhood phase. During the whole of his life, Bernard never had a close, loving relationship with his mother, although he respected her. All the Montgomery children, including Bernard, loved the life in Tasmania. Mount Wellington could be seen from the house and, in another direction, the water of the harbour came into view. In leisure time, there was an outdoor life in the clear air. The Montgomerys' house, called Bishopcourt, was not far from the shore. There were large gardens round the house and the children enjoyed playing in them. In good weather, the family went on outings and had picnics. Swimming, riding and fishing were favourite activities. They made friends with some of the Tasmanian children, and they attended each other's parties.

When Bernard was thirteen, Bishop Montgomery was offered a new post in London. The family sailed from Tasmania and arrived in England in December 1901.

They were coming to England for good, and were to live in a large house at Chiswick, near the centre of London. It was arranged that Bernard and his brother Donald would go to St Paul's School.

At St Paul's, there was one class called 'The Army Class', where boys intending to go into the Army were given a special course. All the new boys, including Bernard, were asked if they wanted to enter the Army Class. Without hesitating, Bernard said he did. He didn't wait to discuss the matter with his parents first, as he should have done. There was no tradition of a military career in either of his parents' families. Bernard had previously shown no desire to become a soldier. Did he answer without thinking? Did he realise how he was committing himself? Was he, as usual, doing just as he wanted? Was he trying to break away from the strict family discipline?

Whatever the answer, Bernard had made a decision which was to affect his whole life. His parents were not pleased to hear what he had done. His father was disappointed, but since Bernard was obstinate and would not withdraw his decision, it was accepted. His mother was very upset, as Bernard knew she would be. There was a heated argument between them, but, in the end, Bernard had his own way. He had entered what was, at that time, regarded as an easy option, the course demanding the least academic effort. Even so, Bernard was lazy and did not work at his lessons. Perhaps this was, in some ways, understandable. The Montgomery children did not go to school in Tasmania, but had tutors who taught them at home, and Bernard was already fifteen years old when he went to St Paul's.

With sport it was different. He excelled at sports he had never known in Tasmania. Donald, his brother, was the school's swimming captain, and Bernard soon earned himself a place in the team. Later, Bernard became the captain of both the Rugger XV and the Cricket First XI. He liked this a lot better than merely being the member of a team. It gave him power to direct and control others. His teams were devoted to their captain, but Bernard Montgomery was known to be ruthless and even vicious when it came to dealing

Setting out to cycle to school (aged seventeen).

with opposing players.

Being in the Army Class, Bernard would be expected to enter the Royal Military College at Sandhurst (now called the Royal Military Academy) on leaving school, and train to be an army officer. In order to gain entry to the Royal Military College, he would have to pass an examination. Suddenly, realising that he was wasting time, Bernard began to work very hard. He proved that, beneath his lazy exterior, he was very intelligent. He sat the examination and passed — at the first attempt. It was a good pass, not merely a scrape. Bernard Law Montgomery was placed seventy-second out of a total of one hundred and seventy accepted entrants to Sandhurst. His training as a military officer was about to begin.

2   The Making of a Soldier

Bernard Montgomery became a cadet at the Royal Military College, Sandhurst, in January 1907. He did well at first, but there were problems. For example, neither he nor his family realised how much money it would cost.

The Sandhurst Rugby team.
Bernard is in the middle row, second from the right.

College fees had to be paid. Bernard was given money for this by his mother, and in addition his parents gave him an allowance of £24 a year — about 50p a week. While this amount would buy very much more in 1907 than today, it was barely enough to cover Bernard's expenses as an army officer in training. Bernard was eager to gain promotion. At that time, the army was not fully mechanised, and the crack regiments were the cavalry regiments, whose soldiers were mounted on horseback. He wanted to go into the cavalry, but he could not afford to, because all cavalry soldiers were required to buy and pay for the upkeep of their own horse.

One thing made up for this lack of money. Bernard had only been at Sandhurst for five weeks when he was promoted to Lance-Corporal. He was put in charge of the group of junior cadets known as B Company. Bernard enjoyed the power of leading others, but he led them into trouble. In the same way as he was disobedient at home, he did things at Sandhurst that were not allowed, and bullied those who crossed him.

There was rivalry between the different companies and some rough practical joking took place. Bernard led B Company not only in bullying, but in carrying out some vicious attacks on other cadets.

Under Montgomery's leadership B Company became a gang of thugs. Instead of showing a good example by obeying army rules, Montgomery arranged attacks on A Company. Pokers and similar articles were used as weapons. Sometimes the victims were hurt, but Bernard Montgomery didn't seem to care.

15

One day, he went too far. Bernard made B Company hold down a member of another company, and then set fire to the young man's clothes. This was no practical joke. The cadet was so badly burned that he had to be admitted to hospital. When questioned, the victim refused to say who had set him alight, but the staff at the Military College knew. Bernard was in disgrace. It looked as if he would be expelled from Sandhurst and his army career would never begin.

His mother was appalled when she learned what her son had done. She realised that this kind of bad behaviour would not only affect Bernard. If Bernard was expelled, disgrace would also fall on his father, the Bishop.

Mrs Montgomery made an appointment to see the Commandant of the College and travelled to meet him. She pleaded with him not to expel Bernard. The Commandant was doubtful. If Bernard behaved so badly, would he ever be fit to be in charge of soldiers? Mrs Montgomery explained how expulsion would shame the whole family, especially her husband.

Eventually the Commandant agreed to let Bernard continue. There would have to be other appropriate punishment. Bernard was stripped of his rank. He was no longer a Lance-Corporal but, once again, a lowly cadet. In addition, he would have to stay at Sandhurst for an extra term in order to complete the course.

The effect of the punishment on Bernard was noticeable straight away. He stopped being a bully and worked very hard. His aim was to get into the Indian Army.

Lieutenant B. L. Montgomery in India, 1910.

*　　*　　*

India was, at that time, still occupied by Britain. A permanent force of soldiers was sent there from England to keep the peace. Officers who served in India were able to live on their pay without help from home. Bernard did not want to ask his family to support him once he was an army officer.

Examination time came and Bernard did his very best. The results showed that he was placed thirty-sixth out of one hundred and fifty. It was not quite good enough. He tried to overcome his disappointment and joined the Royal Warwickshire Regiment.

Then something happened which fulfilled Bernard's wish. One battalion of the Royal Warwickshire Regiment was sent to serve on the North-West Frontier

17

of India. Lieutenant Bernard Montgomery was now an officer in this battalion. At the beginning of his military career he was, after all, to serve in India, though not with the Indian Army.

There were some parts of army life in India that Bernard liked and some that he did not. He enjoyed the sport, and played hockey in addition to cricket. He even bought a horse called 'Probyn'. It had previously been a baggage horse. It was certainly not a racehorse and Montgomery was not an accomplished rider, but he mounted his horse and they won a race. He soon became the Officer in charge of Regimental Sports.

He disliked the regimental dinners that every officer was required to attend. He did not normally smoke or drink alcohol, and felt very ill at ease on social occasions. This dislike of social life continued to some extent throughout his life. He often refused to go to weddings, although he gladly attended ceremonies given in his honour. For his own guests, he provided excellent food and wine, while he ate only plain food and drank water.

Montgomery's ambition was to do well as a soldier. He studied military matters as much as he could. He even learned two very difficult local languages, Urdu and Pushtu, so that he could speak to the Indian soldiers under his command.

The Regiment was recalled to England in January 1913 and Bernard Montgomery was posted to Shorncliffe, near Folkestone. Here he attended a course on the use of weapons, and passed examinations in subjects including the use of the machine-gun and the rifle. He also became friendly with another officer, Captain Lefroy. The two men often talked together. Captain Lefroy made Bernard realise that it was not sufficient for a military man to learn how to use weapons. It was important to study the problems of war and to plan campaigns with cunning and skill.

In July 1914, it became clear that Britain was soon to be at war with Germany. In Europe, the Austro-Hungarian Empire had claimed the state of Bosnia. This was not liked by Russia. When the heir to Austria-Hungary visited the capital of Bosnia, he was shot dead. War between Austria-Hungary and Russia crept ever nearer. Soon Austria-Hungary, supported by Germany, was fighting Russia and her allies, Serbia and France.

Germany invaded Belgium, a country not involved

First World War soldiers in the trenches.

In the 9th Army Corps, France 1917.

in the war, in order to attack France. At this point Great Britain entered the war on the side of France, Russia and Serbia. The British armed forces were mobilised ready for action. There was not long to prepare. World War One was declared on 4th August 1914. At Shorncliffe, the officers were instructed to take their swords to be sharpened by the regimental armourer. Montgomery was puzzled. The swords had so far only been used in ceremonies. Now it was clear that they would be used to fight battles. Bernard had not received any training in how to use a sword.

Within three weeks the Royal Warwickshire Regiment was sent to Belgium. Soon Bernard Montgomery was involved in the fighting. On 8th September, only three weeks after Bernard had landed on the Continent, Bishop Montgomery received a telegram from the War Office. The news was grim. Bernard was reported missing.

But Bishop Montgomery's son was still alive. He had, so far, not been taken prisoner or come to any harm in the warfare. The battalion had taken part in one attack that had failed, and was then ordered to fight at the battle of Ypres.

Montgomery, holding his sword in readiness, led his platoon of thirty men. A group of German soldiers was soon encountered. One was about to shoot Montgomery. Bernard knew that the cumbersome sword was no defence, so he dropped it and kicked the German as hard as he could. The man fell to the ground and Montgomery took him as his first prisoner.

The next time, Montgomery was not so fortunate.

While he and his men were trying to retake a village, a German sniper shot him in the chest and knee. One of Montgomery's men ran to help him and to attend to his wounds, only to be shot and killed by the Germans. The dead soldier fell on top of Montgomery. His body served as protection from the German bullets as the enemy went on firing.

It was hours before things quietened down and members of the British platoon were able to get to the two men. Since both were thought to be dead, graves had been dug for them. Montgomery stirred. He was still alive, but badly wounded.

It took a long time for Bernard to recover, and all his life his damaged lung proved to be troublesome. While he was still in hospital in England, he received important news. For his gallantry during the fighting he was awarded the D.S.O. — the Distinguished Service Order medal — and promoted to the rank of Captain.

When World War One ended on 11th November 1918, Montgomery was a very different person from the one he was when it began. This slight, wiry man with piercing eyes was steady, reliable and trustworthy. He demanded very high standards of himself and others, and was enthusiastic and far-sighted. He also knew there was a need for new methods to be used in military planning. The old form of rows of opposing enemies confronting each other in battle was no longer effective. In future, Montgomery reasoned, the need would be to overcome any enemy by stealth and surprise, and battles would be won by attacking the opponent's weakest point.

3 The Family Man

It was peace-time again and, like most other officers in the regular army, Montgomery was given a rank lower than the one he held during the war. He became a Major.

First, he was posted to Lillers in France. When the soldiers at this base were sent back to England to return to civilian life, Montgomery went to Cologne in Germany. Here he helped as the city settled down to a peace-time existence. Montgomery knew that this work would not last long and that he, too, would return to England. What would happen to him then? His future in the army seemed uncertain.

One thing Montgomery wanted to do was to attend a course at the Staff College at Camberley. It was there,

The Staff College at Camberley.

he thought, that modern military tactics were studied and discussed. He applied for admission three times before he was accepted.

When Montgomery, now aged thirty-two, began his studies at Camberley, he was disappointed. This was the place which was supposed to train top-quality, high-ranking army officers of the future. He did not think this was being done. He felt that much more attention should be given to the study of military matters and less time spent on social occasions. He was very critical of what went on and was sometimes disliked because of the views he expressed.

Bernard worked hard and attended the lectures that were given. He completed the course successfully, but no one told him how well or how badly he had done during the year. This annoyed him. When he left Camberley at the end of the course, he was sent to the 17th Infantry Brigade, a peace-keeping force in Cork, Ireland. There was much trouble in Ireland. At that time, the whole country was ruled by England, but civil war was raging because many Irish people wanted home rule. Montgomery's ancestral home was at Moville in Ireland. This put him in a difficult position, but as he was in Ireland as an officer of the British Army, he carried out his duties.

A truce was reached in Ireland and Montgomery returned to England. He had three postings before becoming an instructor at the Staff College at Camberley — the place where, not long before, he had been a student. The appointment was for three years. It was enough time in which to circulate his ideas.

Betty Montgomery (formerly Carver) in 1927.

Before taking up his appointment at Camberley in January 1926, Montgomery had a winter holiday in Lenk, Switzerland. Here he met Mrs Betty Carver and her two sons. Richard was aged eleven and John thirteen. Betty was a widow. Her husband had been killed at the battle of Gallipoli in World War One. Betty was a calm, cheerful person. Her hobby was art, and she enjoyed painting pictures and portraits, and sculpting figures, but above all she devoted herself to bringing up her two sons.

When she took them on holiday to Lenk, Bernard Montgomery helped Richard and John to learn to ski, and so got to know the family. They all spent a similar holiday there twelve months later.

Betty and Bernard fell in love and were married in July 1927. They were delighted when, a year later, a son was born. Betty, Bernard, Richard and John, together with the new baby, David, were a very happy family.

Bernard took a pride in running his household as smoothly as possible. He organised everything in an almost military manner, from paying bills to making arrangements for guests. He even ordered the groceries, a task normally undertaken at that time by the wife. Above all, he did not neglect Betty's two elder boys, but took care of them.

Betty with her two older sons, Richard and John,
and baby David (Montgomery's son).

Montgomery's military career still progressed. After Camberley he was posted to Woking and given the task of revising the Army's Infantry Training Manual. In this he included many of his own ideas. Some army officers wanted to make amendments to the new Manual, but Montgomery, with his usual obstinacy, refused to let anything be altered.

Early in 1931, the first battalion of the Royal Warwickshire Regiment was posted abroad. With them Montgomery went to Palestine, Alexandria in Egypt and Quetta in India. Betty joined him at various times and Richard, John and David visited them on different occasions.

During Montgomery's periods of leave, visits were made to Singapore, Japan, China and other interesting places. Betty and David were with Montgomery in Quetta when a very severe earthquake occurred. He sent them back to England for safety.

Soon Montgomery, now a Brigadier, was posted to Portsmouth. He had to go away on army exercises on Salisbury Plain. While he was there, Betty and David had a holiday in Burnham-on-Sea.

David and his mother were on the beach one day when Betty's foot was bitten by an insect. That night her foot and leg began to swell and become very painful. The doctor was called and immediately arranged for Betty to be taken to hospital. Bernard was sent for.

Things did not improve. When Montgomery arrived, the infection had spread to the whole of Betty's body and blood poisoning had set in. At this time, penicillin

Montgomery and David in Switzerland, 1937.

and other antibiotics had not been discovered — doctors
did not know how to overcome the illness. Montgomery
tried to believe that it was only a matter of time before
all would be well again, but Betty became worse. She
died on 19th October 1937.

Montgomery was stunned. Their marriage was so
happy. Betty and he had been together for just ten
years. For days, even weeks, he refused to see anyone.
He wanted to be alone with his grief.

Suddenly, he determined that he must overcome his
sorrow. He must pursue his military career again.

4 Dunkirk and After

Montgomery worked hard at his military duties in an attempt to overcome the grief caused by his wife's death. Soon the 9th Infantry Brigade, with Montgomery in command, became one of the British Army's top brigades.

The following year, in October 1938, Montgomery was promoted to the rank of Major-General and posted to Palestine. The shadow of war soon fell on Europe. Concern had been felt during the 1930s as the German

Hitler enters the Reichstag to deliver a speech.

National Socialist Party, the Nazis, gained strength. In 1933, Adolf Hitler became Chancellor of the German state, the Reich. He promised to make Germany a great nation. He declared that Jews and Communists were preventing the country's rise to power. They must be dealt with. He caused the Jews and his political opponents to be cruelly treated. They were put into labour camps and prisons where, more often than not, they died.

Hitler was ruthless. Germany began to manufacture large quantities of war equipment and ammunition. It became clear that Hitler intended to conquer other countries by attacking them. The German troops over-ran Austria, and then invaded and claimed control of Czechoslovakia.

On 1st September 1939, Hitler's army entered Poland. Both Britain and France had signed treaties with Poland, promising to help if that country was attacked. These treaties were honoured, and on 3rd September 1939, both Britain and France declared war on Germany. Russia joined with Germany to honour a treaty.

World War Two had begun. Britain and France were allies fighting against Germany and Russia. British troops made ready to fight on French soil.

Only six days before the war began, Montgomery was given the command of the 3rd Division of the Army. Before crossing the English Channel with his men to join the British Expeditionary Force, he made arrangements for his young son David to be cared for by friends.

Wehrmacht anti-aircraft guns in Holland.

Montgomery's 3rd Division was stationed at Lille in the north of France. There was no encounter with the enemy during the whole of the winter. The British troops spent the time undergoing rigorous training.

Then, on 10th May 1940, the Germans invaded Belgium and Holland. Montgomery and the 3rd Division were ordered to leave Lille and move eastwards to Belgium. France was also attacked, and German forces swept across the country towards the capital, Paris. This was serious. Hitler was trying to conquer the whole of Europe. There was now the threat that, after France, Germany would attempt to invade and conquer England.

French and British forces were split as the Germans advanced from the south. The enemy captured the French towns of Calais and Boulogne. The British forces were trapped. The only hope of escape was to retreat to the French port of Dunkirk, which was not yet in German hands.

On the night of 27th/28th May 1940, Belgium surrendered. Montgomery, now in command of the large 2nd Corps, was in a difficult position. With great skill he moved his men by night across the line of the attacking enemy to a new position. Eventually, after marching many miles, they joined the queues of other exhausted soldiers waiting on the sandy Dunkirk beaches. Montgomery gave the final order for withdrawal. The men were to be ferried across the Channel to England.

Sailing craft of every kind drew alongside the

Evacuation from Dunkirk in May 1940.

retreating Army, dodging the heavy German fire. Under the protection of the British Navy, six hundred and fifty vessels of all types sailed back and forth across the sea in the rescue attempt. Many of these boats were small and were never intended to cross the English Channel. Tiny holiday craft, pleasure steamers and motor boats all played their part. Because of the heavy bombing, not all returned to England. All of them did magnificent work in the attempt to rescue the retreating soldiers. As the operation drew to a close, Montgomery boarded a Royal Navy destroyer at dawn on 1st June 1940. He arrived safely at Dover later that day. Dunkirk was a major defeat, but it was a miracle that so many of the forces were rescued.

Montgomery was now acknowledged to be an outstanding army leader. His men of the 3rd Division were re-formed and prepared in readiness to return to France. Before they could do so, France surrendered. There was now only Britain to face the enemy. To make matters worse, in May 1940 Italy had entered the war on the side of Germany.

England was threatened more than ever. The country had to be defended against possible invasion. Montgomery had his own plan of action. He placed a line of troops along the South-east coast. Larger formations of soldiers were positioned further inland, ready to go to any area where help was needed. Montgomery made sure that all communications were good, whether by telephone, radio or road. Everything had to be in perfect order. Not only that, his men had to be physically fit.

Montgomery was very strict. When he gave a lecture to his men, he allowed two minutes before he began for anyone to cough. After that, coughing was forbidden. Smoking was not allowed during lectures, and if anyone arrived late, he was not admitted until the break half way through. Because of the thoroughness of Montgomery's training, his troops were ready to protect the country against invasion.

The war was fought on many fronts. In addition to the conflict in Europe, fighting was taking place in other countries. Hitler sent one of his best forces, the Afrika Korps, to fight in North Africa.

When Hitler invaded Russia in 1941, Russia changed sides and became an ally of Britain. In 1942, the United States of America began to take a full part in World War Two as one of Britain's allies. It was then that the Japanese attacked Pearl Harbour, the United States Naval base on one of the Hawaiian Islands in the Pacific Ocean, and the conflict became world-wide. Until that time, the United States had been supplying Britain with weapons, but American troops had not taken any part in the fighting. All that changed, and both America and Russia now joined the fight against Germany.

In August 1942, Montgomery travelled to Scotland, where a big army exercise was to take place. Not long after he arrived, a call was received from the War Office. He was to return to London at once in order to take a command in operation 'Torch'. In this operation, planned for the autumn, British and American forces were to land in North Africa, where the war was not going well for the Allies. Montgomery was to be in command of the Northern Task Force under General Eisenhower, the American who was later to become the United States President.

Montgomery's appointment was never taken up. Early the next morning, he received another call from the War Office. General Gott, who had been ordered to be in charge of the Eighth Army stationed in Africa, had been killed in a plane crash. Lieutenant-General Bernard Montgomery was to take his place, and become one of the most famous British Army Commanders of all time.

Lieutenant-General Montgomery
arrives to take command of the 8th Army in Cairo.

5 The Desert Rats

Montgomery arrived in Cairo on 12th August 1942 and travelled to his headquarters in the desert. He was to take charge of the whole of the Eighth Army. He was now in command of a modern army in battle. General Gott had been killed before he had been able to take up his duties, so Montgomery took over the command from General Auchinleck, who had been in charge.

He lost no time in beginning his work. He found that things were in a poor way. The soldiers were down-hearted. Since January, the Germans had pushed the Eighth Army back six hundred miles, sweeping across North Africa from west to east. There were suggestions that further retreat was likely. Hitler's Afrika Korps seemed to be much the better force.

Montgomery in his caravan flanked by pictures of
Rommel (left) and Himmler.

One of the first things Montgomery did was to cancel all orders connected with a possible withdrawal. He inspected his headquarters. He looked at a framework of scaffolding-like pipes over which was draped a fine mosquito net, intended to keep out the insects. This was where the former commander had taken his meals. 'What's this?' cried Montgomery, 'a meat-safe?' (Before refrigerators were in common use, meat was often kept in a little cupboard called a meat-safe. The sides and doors were made of thin metal pierced with hundreds of tiny holes. This was so that air could circulate round the meat inside, but flies and blue-bottles could not get in.)

Montgomery was not going to live in the huge, ungainly structure which was no protection from the hot desert sun. 'Take it down,' he ordered.

Without delay, Montgomery moved his headquarters to Burg el Arab. Here the communications were better. He obtained three caravans and worked from these. In one of them he hung pictures of three of his high-ranking German enemies, including Rommel. Field-Marshal Erwin Rommel was in command of German and Italian forces in North Africa. Montgomery was determined to defeat him.

He tried to make things better for the soldiers. Since they were near to the sea, those who wished were allowed to swim. Before Montgomery arrived the officers and the troops lived in the open air, eating in the hot sun and sleeping on the ground. Work which could not be done in the open air was carried out in the few trucks which were available. He permitted tents to be erected because he wanted everyone to be reasonably comfortable.

Despite his stern orders and what some regarded as his peculiar ways, Montgomery was very popular with the troops, who called him 'Monty'. They liked the way he visited them regularly, improved their conditions and kept them informed of the military position.

It was different with officers. Montgomery was high-handed and often chose to ignore a senior officer. He could be quite ruthless with officers who served under him. If an officer did not come up to his high standards, the man would be told that he was useless. Montgomery did not hesitate to dismiss those who did not satisfy his requirements. There was a lot of jealousy, too, when Montgomery's unusual methods were successful. His fellow officers did not like his troops always proving to be the best trained. Certainly, he could be curt and rude to those who opposed him or did not win his approval.

He regularly inspected the Eighth Army soldiers. When he visited a unit of Australian soldiers, one of the officers suggested that he might like to wear an Australian soldier's slouch hat. Montgomery did. He not only wore it then, but whenever he visited his troops. He also pinned to it the badge of every unit he visited. He thought it was a good way for him to be recognised by his men. Some time after, he was in an armoured tank watching fighting taking place. The big hat got in the way, and he was given a more suitable tank beret. This pleased him, and he pinned his own officer's badge next to that of the Royal Tank Corps.

Wearing his Australian hat, Monty greets the
Commander of the Greek Brigade in the 8th Army.

He was often seen wearing his black beret afterwards,
although it was not an official part of his uniform.

Foremost in Montgomery's mind were his plans to
defeat Rommel, the brilliant German General who was
known as 'The Desert Fox'. Montgomery was sure that
his carefully thought out campaign would bring victory.
The enemy was still advancing. Montgomery positioned
his tanks and forces on a ridge of high ground called
Alam el Halfa. He waited until the enemy was passing
between marshy land on one side and Alam el Halfa
ridge on the other, and then attacked. The battle was a
long one, lasting from 31st August to 6th September
1942.

Because of British minefields, the enemy progress was slow at first. Then the Germans had to take a different route, resulting in an encounter with more British troops. The British tanks were well dug in and held on. Finally, when the Germans were desperately short of petrol, Rommel ordered a retreat. One famous Allied contingent which took part in the fighting was the 7th Armoured Division, known as 'The Desert Rats'. (The animal called the jerboa is the actual desert rat. It is a small creature with a tufted tail and, because its hind legs are much longer than its front legs, it can leap a long way. In 1940, the wife of the Commander of the 7th Armoured Division suggested to her husband that his men should wear a circular badge showing a little red jerboa on a white background. Soon the Desert Rats became famous for their service in North Africa.)

Montgomery intended to attack at El Alamein. This city was in the north and the Mediterranean coastline was only a few miles away. It was important not to let the enemy know anything about the plan of attack. In order to confuse Rommel, Montgomery had imitation pipelines laid in the south. It was hoped that the enemy would think that these pipelines were intended to supply petrol and water to the British troops attacking from the south. These deceptions caused the Germans to calculate that the Allied forces would attack in mid-November. Montgomery had no intention of waiting as long as that.

Rommel was a sick man. He needed treatment for a stomach complaint. The Desert Fox judged that he would have time to travel by air to Austria for medical attention before the Allied forces attacked.

Montgomery's men were ready and well-prepared. They were promised victory as they went forward to destroy Rommel. On the night of 23rd/24th October 1942, when the moon was full, Montgomery's Eighth Army attacked in the north in order to regain El Alamein. The battle was fought with armoured tanks and artillery across hazardous minefields. It was difficult. Soon the attack switched to the weakest area of the enemy line. The final attack, named 'Supercharge', began. Rommel, who had flown back from Austria on receiving news of the battle, gave the order to withdraw. General von Thoma, who was in charge of the famous Afrika Korps, surrendered to Montgomery.

On 4th November 1942, the Battle of El Alamein was over. Montgomery had won a magnificent victory. Not only was it a great achievement, it was the turning point of World War Two.

When the news reached Britain, the Prime Minister, Winston Churchill, instructed that church bells all over the country should be rung in celebration. Until now, during the war, the bells had been silent, with the command that they were only to be rung as a warning in case of invasion. The whole country rejoiced as the bells were allowed to peal, marking the victory of El Alamein.

Monty was honoured by being knighted, and became General Sir Bernard Montgomery.

6 Monty's Double

Montgomery was very cautious. After the defeat of Rommel's forces at the Battle of El Alamein, he could have continued fighting until he had forced the enemy out of North Africa. However, he knew his men were weary. Before beginning any further action, it was essential to check supplies, to gather together his tanks and artillery and to make careful plans. Montgomery never went into battle until everything was ready.

The fight went on across Libya. Tripoli was captured and the enemy defeated at the Battle of the Mareth Line. The Eighth Army was now in Tunisia. Soon the three ports of Gabes, Sfax and Sousse were taken. It was not easy. Rommel made numerous strong counter-attacks.

Taking delivery of the B-17 'Flying Fortress'.

The Eighth Army joined up with the American forces. Montgomery had to work alongside the commanders of the United States Army. Relations were not always easy. In particular, he did not get on with the American General, George Patton. Montgomery did not rate the United States forces very highly. They had not experienced much fighting and he felt that they were not battle-hardened like his own soldiers. General Eisenhower was now the Commander-in-Chief of all the Allied Forces.

It was at Sfax where the link-up of Allied and American forces was to take place. When the battle was being planned, one of Eisenhower's staff told Montgomery that if he could take Sfax by a given date, he would be given a United States flying-fortress bomber aircraft, complete with an eight-man crew. Montgomery arrived at Sfax five days earlier than the agreed date. He asked for his reward, only to be told that it was all a joke. Montgomery insisted. The aircraft was given to him, but the episode did not help good relations.

The fight against the German army continued. After many difficulties, a victorious British Eighth Army led the American First Army into the conquered city of Tunis. It signified victory over the enemy and the end of the North Africa Campaign.

During April and early May 1943, plans were made to invade Sicily, the little island in the Mediterranean Sea just off the toe of Italy. The area where the North African Campaign had recently ended was not far across the water. Although Montgomery's forces played a major part in the fighting, it was General Patton's American troops who made a rapid thrust in the north of the island and gave the Allies the victory.

This did not please Montgomery. Although Sicily was now in Allied hands, Montgomery was cross about the way it had been captured. General Patton had first captured the large city of Palermo and then rapidly moved to the other part of the island, near to Italy, and taken Messina. Montgomery felt that it was a mistake for the American General to have wasted time in capturing Palermo. He reasoned that this allowed the German forces to escape to Italy. Montgomery planned to capture the Germans in Sicily, make them prisoners of war, and prevent them continuing to fight against the Allies.

The next onslaught was on the mainland of Italy. Italy is difficult mountainous country, but at first things went well. The Italians were soon beaten and signed an armistice early in September 1943. They did not take any more part in the war, but the Germans went on fighting on Italian soil.

On Christmas Eve 1943, Montgomery received an unexpected order to return to England. He was to help to plan the invasion of Europe. The code-name for the European operation was 'Overlord'. General Eisenhower of the United States was in overall command. Immediately under him was General Sir Bernard Montgomery. Monty was responsible for the 21st Army Group, whose armies included British, American and Canadian troops. The planning of the invasion began without delay. The enemy must not suspect what was going on. Various ploys were used to deceive the Germans.

It was discovered that there was an officer who looked very much like Montgomery. Lieutenant Clifton James was on war service with the Royal Army Pay Corps. In civilian life, Lieutenant James was an actor. It was arranged that he should impersonate Montgomery. He studied Monty's mannerisms, the way he stood and the way he walked, in order to improve the look-alike. At last, Lieutenant James was ready to play the part.

Lieutenant James wore a uniform which was an exact

Monty drives down a street in Birmingham which has been named after him.

copy of Montgomery's. It had the correct badges of rank and rows of ribbons representing the medals which Montgomery had won. Most importantly, Lieutenant James wore a black Tank Corp beret, with two badges attached to it, exactly as Montgomery did.

A bomber aircraft flew Monty's double to Gibraltar. He was received and given a meal. All the honour normally shown to the real General was given to Lieutenant Clifton James. The next day he was flown to Algiers. He held several meetings which, since he was heard to mention 'Plan 303', were supposed to deal with military matters. Monty's double also presided over several army ceremonies.

The German Intelligence followed Montgomery's movements with great interest. As usual, they noted that 'Montgomery' travelled around, regularly visiting his troops. Did they wonder whether his plan was to attack the south of France? In reality, they had seen Lieutenant Clifton James, Monty's double.

But there was one big difference between Bernard Montgomery and his double. While Monty did not smoke or drink, Lieutenant Clifton James was fond of doing both. Whenever Clifton James had a meal with other officers and important people, he could not resist the opportunity to have a drink. It was not at all in keeping with the character of the real Montgomery. The impersonation was spoiled. It could not be long before the watchful German agents guessed the truth. Operation 'Copperhead', the name by which the deception was known, was soon brought to a close and Lieutenant Clifton James sent back to England.

46

7 D-Day

All this time, the real Monty stayed in England, busily planning the invasion of Europe. Preparations were made all over Britain. Not only did the armed forces undergo rigorous training, but the manufacture of war vehicles, arms and ammunition was stepped up. Montgomery was keen to include new types of vehicles and inventions in his army, a decision which, later on, proved to be a very wise one. There were tanks which could operate on water, bulldozers with strong armour to protect them, and tanks with chains attached to a drum on the front of the vehicle. These chains, called flails, made mines explode before the tank ran over

Eisenhower (on left) and Monty plan D-Day.

them. All this equipment, and vast quantities of food and other supplies, had to be landed on the continent without alerting the enemy.

The numerous army vehicles would need fuel during the fighting in France. For this purpose, a pipeline under the ocean (nicknamed PLUTO from the initial letters of the words) was built under the English Channel. Montgomery arranged that, once the troops had landed, artificial harbours called 'Mulberry' harbours would be built out of pre-formed sections. He also planned to use FIDO, a method of dispersing fog from the landing areas. Montgomery was ready to take advantage of any invention which he was sure would help his men to gain victory.

Monty became a national hero. Not only did he inspire his troops, but civilians as well. He made everyone feel that they had their part to play in defeating Hitler.

England became a secret store for the planned invasion. Long stretches of coastline were sealed off. Supplies of ammunition were hidden in forests and new tanks were secreted beneath trees which shaded stretches of grassland. These were not haphazard stores — everything was in its place ready for the invasion.

At last the plan was ready. General Eisenhower was in overall charge of the Allied land, sea and air forces. He was the Supreme Commander. Montgomery had hoped that he would be chosen for the post since he had led his forces to such outstanding victories in North Africa. He was disappointed that the American had been given the senior appointment in preference to him. General Sir Bernard Montgomery was the Ground Force Commander responsible for all the allied troops who fought on land.

D-Day and H-Hour had to be fixed. 'D' stood for the *D*ay and 'H' for the *H*our when Europe would be attacked. D-Day was to be either the 5th, 6th or 7th June, 1944. Bad weather delayed the action on the 5th. The weather forecast was good for the 6th and the decision was taken to invade the Normandy beaches on that day.

During 5th June and on the morning of 6th June, the air force made preliminary raids to destroy enemy radar stations and disrupt enemy road and rail communications. On the morning of 5th June, the fleet carrying the troops gathered off the Isle of Wight. As evening drew near and the light began to fade, the

Troops surge onto the Normandy beaches.

troops sailed. The main bulk of their supplies followed close behind. Accompanying ships searched the seas for enemy submarines and warships. Fifteen convoys of fighter planes protected the men sailing to invade Normandy.

The Allied forces arrived on the Normandy shores at dawn on D-Day, 6th June 1944. H-Hour, when the attack began, varied from 6.30 a.m. to 7.45 a.m. at different landing points, according to the tide.

Montgomery's plan was to divide the Normandy coastline into five sections. The British army would land on the beaches which Montgomery code-named Sword, Juno and Gold, while the Americans would land at beaches with the code-names Omaha and Utah. The forces landed and by the 10th June a strip of territory sixty miles long and about ten miles wide had been taken. It was not easy. The enemy bombarded the soldiers as they went ashore. Land mines had been buried in the beaches and when these blew up they delayed and sometimes destroyed the tanks and vehicles.

Montgomery did not only follow events from a safe distance in England. On 8th June, two days after D-Day, he visited the invasion beaches in France to see how Operation Overlord was progressing.

After the Canadians lost ground at one point, reports were issued suggesting that all was not well and that the Allied forces could make no headway at all. Much of the criticism was made against Montgomery. Again there was friction between him and the American officers. It was only because Winston Churchill, England's Prime Minister, and General Alan Brooke, the Chief of the Imperial General Staff, did not lose their confidence in Montgomery that he still held his command.

The battles continued. Eventually the Canadians succeeded in reaching and taking Falaise. The Falaise Gap was closed sufficiently to trap most of the Germans fighting there. The remnant of the German army fled. Rommel was wounded and later committed suicide. The Allies fought on and liberated Paris, the capital of France, on 25th August 1944.

Montgomery's plan had been successful. It was his greatest victory.

On 1st September 1944, Montgomery was promoted to the highest rank in the British army. He was made a Field-Marshal. The honour was somewhat overshadowed when General Eisenhower promoted General Bradley and made him equal to Montgomery. No longer had Montgomery sole command of all the ground forces. He was now only in charge of the 21st Army Group.

Prime Minister Churchill and Monty in north-west France, July 1944.

51

8 The Conquest of Europe

The Allied soldiers pushed the Nazi troops out of Belgium and Holland, and then continued across France. Eisenhower's plan was to attack on all fronts. Montgomery would have preferred to make a single thrust at the enemy's weakest point, but he did not have the authority to choose what to do.

The war did not always go smoothly. The Germans fought back in the Ardennes region, and many of General Bradley's American soldiers were killed. The situation worsened. General Eisenhower knew only one man who could turn the defeat into a victory — Montgomery. He asked the British Field-Marshal to take over the command of two of the United States armies. Eventually, the enemy was routed and the Allies could advance.

Unfortunately, during the action, Montgomery offended General Eisenhower by writing to ask that one officer should command *all* the British and American troops now under his own and General Bradley's command. This suggestion was very much out of place. Montgomery was telling the Supreme Commander — the officer who was above him — what he ought to do. It was not the first time that he had shown a lack of tact. Fortunately, Montgomery apologised before it was too late, and asked Eisenhower to tear up his letter.

General Eisenhower bore no grudge against Montgomery. When the Battle of the Ardennes had been won, he asked Montgomery to continue to command one of the two United States Armies which had been under his temporary control.

In the early months of 1945, the war in Europe reached its climax. While General Alexander fought the Germans in Italy, the Russian Allies pressed on to reach Berlin, the Americans crossed the River Rhine, and Montgomery with his forces swept on across North West Germany. Soon the British, American and Russian forces linked up. Fighting continued in the German Rhineland.

The important city of Hamburg was captured by the Allies. A group of defeated German Officers led by Admiral Friedeburg was taken to Lüneburg Heath, where Montgomery had his Headquarters. The officers were prepared to surrender their own armies. Montgomery would not accept. It was not enough. He demanded that they surrender to him all the German forces in the territory for which he was responsible. At first the Germans refused. Montgomery left them to think the matter over, and then set a deadline. Just

Reading the terms of surrender at Lüneburg Heath, 1945.

before the time of the deadline was reached, the Germans agreed to unconditional surrender. On 4th May 1945, in a tent near to Montgomery's caravan, the document called the Instrument of Surrender was signed by Montgomery and the German Officers. Montgomery signed on behalf of General Eisenhower but did not forward the document to him. He kept that for himself, and sent Eisenhower a copy. The original Instrument of Surrender is now in the Imperial War Museum in London. The surrender was a major achievement for Montgomery and the fulfilment of his main ambition. The war in Europe was over.

*   *   *

Much needed to be done. There was now no effective Government in Germany. The Allies — British, French, American and Russian — divided the country into four zones of occupation. Each was responsible for one zone, and Montgomery was appointed Controller of the British zone. With his usual military precision, he began to bring things back to life for the twenty million Germans under his authority. The population included military prisoners and civilian refugees. As usual, Montgomery went to see for himself. He visited a refugee camp and realised that not only here, but all over the British zone, people were weak from the lack of food. Many were in such a poor state of health that an epidemic of disease could easily break out. Montgomery soon had the farms working again and organised the harvesting of grain and food.

Winter was coming. He put the fuel industry back

into production as soon as possible. He made sure that all available supplies were put to the best use. Soon the factories were in operation. Plans were made for the postal services to begin again and for public transport to be restored.

He made strict rules which had to be kept by the occupying British forces. They were not allowed to buy food in the German shops because this was needed to feed the German people. The British Army supplied the needs of the troops. At first, the British soldiers were not allowed to befriend the Germans, but as the country returned to peace-time life, these rules were gradually relaxed.

On 22nd August 1945, while Montgomery was flying to visit Canadian troops in Germany, his aircraft crashed so badly that it was a write-off. Although at first it seemed that Montgomery was only shaken, it was soon found that two bones in his spine had been damaged. He recovered, but remained very weak. Early the following year, in January 1946, he became very ill with influenza and a lung infection. After receiving hospital treatment, he went to Switzerland for a holiday in order to regain his strength. He felt better when he returned.

The winter of 1945-6, the first after the end of the war, was very severe. Because of good administration under the control of Field-Marshal Montgomery, the people in the British zone of Germany did not suffer unduly. Gradually the control of the area was taken over by German civilian officials and peace-time life in the country began.

9 Honours

Monty was a popular hero. His reputation as the Field-Marshal who led his men to victory received wide recognition. A great deal of his time was taken up receiving honours and presentations. In Britain, among other things, he received honorary doctorates from a number of universities and had the freedom of seventeen towns bestowed upon him. European countries were anxious to show their gratitude to him. France, Poland, Denmark, Belgium and Russia were among the countries which made presentations of medals and similar honours to him.

One of the highest awards he was given was in Britain when, in the New Year's Honours List of 1946, it was announced that he was to be made a Viscount. Bernard Law Montgomery became a peer of the realm. He took as his title 'Viscount Montgomery of Alamein'.

Later in January 1946, he was promoted to the highest post in the British Army. He became the Chief of the Imperial General Staff, starting his appointment in June. Members of Parliament were uneasy. Montgomery now had enormous power. Not only was he the Chief of the Imperial General Staff but, as a Viscount, he was also a member of the House of Lords, the Upper House of Parliament. The politicians knew that Montgomery regarded his way as the only right one. They knew, too, that he often did whatever he wished regardless of the way it would affect others.

Montgomery continued to look after the needs of the British soldier. He insisted that the pay and the living conditions of men serving in the army should be improved and that numerous parades which had no purpose should not be held. Although military authority and discipline are essential, Montgomery wanted the troops to be treated as human beings.

As Chief of the Imperial General Staff, he gave instructions relating to the administration of all sections of the army. He wrote a paper entitled *The Problem of the Post-War Army* which set out his opinions on what ought to be done. Although it was peace-time, all young men had to serve in the army for a stated length of time. Montgomery wanted this period to be increased. He also asked for more money to be spent on the armed services.

In retirement at Isington Mill.

In 1948 an invitation was given to Montgomery to become the Chairman of the Western Union Commanders-in-Chief Committee and to take part in forming NATO. NATO (the North Atlantic Treaty Organisation) links the United States, Canada, and ten European nations in planning together the defence of their countries. When NATO was set up, Montgomery became the Deputy Supreme Commander, with the American General Eisenhower in overall control. Among other duties, Montgomery was in charge of the training of all the forces. He held this post for ten years and then retired.

When Portsmouth was bombed in 1941, Montgomery lost all his personal belongings. After that, he had no permanent home. When on leave, he visited Major and Mrs Reynolds. Montgomery's son, David, once attended the school where Major Reynolds was the Headmaster. Major and Mrs Reynolds looked after David while his father was away in the army. The Reynolds lived at Alton in Hampshire and opposite their home was an old mill, Isington Mill. In 1947, Montgomery bought the old mill. It took several years for renovations to be completed, but when Montgomery gave up his NATO appointment in 1958, it was ready for him to set up home.

The famous man did not lead an idle retirement. In addition to writing a number of books about his successful campaigns, he travelled a great deal. He followed sport with interest and supported Portsmouth Football Club. His comments on the sports in which he used to participate were forthright — especially regarding cricket and ski-ing. He kept a wary eye on international matters.

As an army commander, Montgomery had been eager to see to the welfare of young soldiers. In retirement, he took part in furthering the activities of boys' organisations, including the Outward Bound Trust and the National Association of Boys' Clubs. He was delighted when young people came to visit him, and particularly enjoyed the company of his grand-children.

Viscount Montgomery of Alamein still took his place in the House of Lords. At the State Opening of Parliament in 1968, he was given the honour of carrying the ceremonial Sword of State. It was the third time that he had been selected to do this. The heavy sword had to be carried upright during the long procession and then held in this position all the time the Queen was delivering her speech from the throne. Montgomery, now eighty-one years of age, performed the duty perfectly until the Queen began to speak. The cumbersome sword moved slightly from its upright position. A few moments later it swayed noticeably. Montgomery seemed as if he was about to faint. A court official took the sword and held it steadily upright, while others quietly helped Montgomery out of the room and away from the ceremony. He did not take part in public events again.

The sword was the weapon with which he first went into battle at the beginning of active service in World War One. The sword was the last weapon he held as he ceremoniously protected his Queen at the end of his service to his country.

What kind of man did Montgomery turn out to be? His fellow officers found him domineering, inconsiderate and determined to have his own way. Often his way was the right one, but not always. He was idolised by the public and immensely popular with the troops. The soldiers knew he would do his best for them. His plans were carefully made and no undue risks were taken with their lives. Personally he was a rather lonely man who did not get on too well with some members of his family.

But he was fearless and brave; he was a fine commander of men and he was never defeated in a military campaign. He played a major part in leading the Allied forces to victory in World War Two.

None of this is revealed on the plain stone slab which marks his grave. Montgomery died at the age of eighty-eight, having spent several years in quiet retirement. He is buried in the churchyard at Binsted in Hampshire. He had worshipped at the little country church for twenty-five years.

The gravestone lying flat on the ground simply states

Bernard Law

1st Viscount
Montgomery of Alamein
KC   GCB   DSO

Field-Marshal
17th November 1887
24th March 1976

General Montgomery observes operations during the Battle of El Alamein.

61